Cool Clive
and the
Little Pest

Michaela Morgan

Illustrated by Dee Shulman

Chapter 1

4

'Come on. Let's go!' said Mum.

'Now,' said Mum. 'You've got everything you need and Clive is in school with you. He'll look after you...'

My mum is always asking me to do impossible things. She says:

But the next thing she asked me to do was *really* impossible.

If you knew my little sister, you'd know it is not easy keeping her out of trouble.

She's a little pest.

She has always been a little pest.

And she always will be a little pest.

Chapter 2

My little sister, Jade, has been trouble since the day she was born.

I remember the day Mum brought her home from the hospital. I'd been promised a sister who would be fun to play with. I got a red-faced, wrinkled, soggy little bundle.

Everyone adored her...

...and everyone ignored me.

All the time she was a baby I kept
an eye on her.

When she lost things…

…I found them.

When she made a mess…

…I helped clean it up.

When she learnt to walk…

…I caught
her.

And sometimes I felt just a bit fed up.

She has always had annoying habits – like collecting animals.

If she sees a lonely ladybird, she brings it home.

If she sees a wandering worm, she brings it home.

If she sees a slimy snail, she brings it home.

Our house is like a zoo sometimes. Especially when Jade's animals escape.

So you see, she really was a little pest when she was a baby but now that she's five she's...

... a bigger pest.

Still, she is my sister and she does have her good points...

...and so
I agreed to keep an eye on her.

I walked to school with Jade and my mum.

All the way there I kept my eye on her.

I showed them the way to Jade's classroom and I made my promise to Mum.

Chapter 3

When I make a promise I keep it. So
every now and then during the day,
I'd peep into Jade's class. Or I'd pass by
to see how she was.

In the morning, Jade
was having a good time
painting.

I just popped in to keep her out of trouble.

At playtime she made some friends and I kept an eye on her.

At dinnertime I kept an eye on her.

All day long I kept an eye on her.
I helped her find the right line.

I helped her find the right shoes.

I helped her find the right coat…

…and then I took her home.

And she hadn't got into trouble once.

I felt proud of myself.

Chapter 4

It was just as we were going into the house that I noticed something odd. Very odd indeed.

Jade's hat was moving.

It was wriggling and squiggling around on her head as if it was alive.

It was a really bobbly,
bobbing-up-and-down
bobble hat.

And it was making a noise – a

sort of noise.

Was it alive?

I grabbed at it and
pulled it off her head.
And what did I find?

The school hamster.

'I didn't want him to be lonely,' said Jade.

'I didn't want poor Bubble to stay at school all by himself so I brought him home.'

It's all right, he can sleep with my teddies.

She didn't understand she'd done something wrong.

She didn't understand she was in trouble now.

And I had promised to keep an eye on her!

I took Jade into the house and handed her over to Mum. Then I went back to school. I took the hamster with me.

Chapter 5

Jade hadn't meant to steal the
hamster. She was really trying to help.
She just didn't understand. It was up
to me to keep her out of trouble.

I crept into school.

An empty school is a spooky place. It's quiet. It smells of chalk and disinfectant.

There are echoes.  Echoes of footsteps in the distance. Echoes of clangs and bangs.

After a while I realized the noises were made by Mrs Mopping, the caretaker. She was the only person in the school. I crept past her.

I crept through the hall.

I crept through the cloakroom.

And I crept into the classroom.

I popped Bubble, the hamster, back in his cage.

And then I heard something. Someone else was creeping around – and whispering.

I listened. This is what I heard:

They were burglars! Thieves! They'd
come to rob my school!

Chapter 6

What should I do? What should I do? I panicked. I felt shaky and cold with fear. I really felt like running out and screaming, but I had to keep a cool head.

I was too frightened to move, but I had to do something. Then I remembered a lesson we'd had once.

I could dial 999.
Then the police
would come
and help.

Yes!

Now all I
needed was
a phone.

I started to
creep back across
the cloakroom,
back across the
hall – to the
secretary's office
and the phone.

Made it!

I turned the handle of the door.

The door didn't move.

It was locked.

I couldn't hear the mysterious men
– but I knew they must be nearby.

They could be hiding anywhere.
I held my breath and listened
carefully. I could hear something.

It was a sort of clinking,
jangling metal sound.

CLINK CLANK

JANGLE!

SECRETARY

Then I realized what it was.

It was Mrs Mopping.

She was locking up and going home!

I didn't think twice. I just ran towards her.

Mrs. Mopping!

She nearly jumped out of her skin.

Then she began to tell me off.

CLIVE! What do you think you're doing here at this hour.

I stopped her.

I told her as much as
I could, as quickly as I could
and as quietly as I could.
I didn't want the thieves to
hear me.

'We have to keep our cool,' I said, 'and we have to phone the police.'

We crept back to the secretary's office.

Mrs Mopping unlocked the door as quietly as she could, but every sound we made seemed to echo round the school.

We dialled 999.

'Emergency. Which service do you require?' said the operator. 'Police,' we said.

We had to give our names and the address of the school and we were told to stay where we were.

We stayed. We lay low and waited and listened.

Then we heard footsteps.

'Oh my!' said Mrs Mopping.

Chapter 7

We heard the footsteps coming closer.

We heard a **CREAKING** of doors, a **squeaking** of shoes.

Then we heard **THUMPING** and **BUMPING** and **DRAGGING**.

'They've got the stuff!' said Mrs Mopping.

And then we heard something else.

A screech of brakes, a slamming of doors, running feet and then...

...the door to the secretary's office opened.

It was the police.
'Well done,' they said.

You had your wits about you.

The next day at assembly, I had to stand on the stage with Mrs Mopping and a policewoman.

She told everyone what I'd done. She said the teachers had taught us well because I knew how to call the police.

Then Miss Strictly, my teacher, came up on the stage.

'Oh, oh!' I thought. 'Is she going to tell me off again?'

But she said:
'Well done, Clive!
You've saved the day...
...and the computer...
...and the video...
...and the television.'

Everyone clapped and clapped. And no one clapped louder than my little sister, Jade.

I had a great day. I was the star of assembly.

I got to choose the team in football

and the dinner ladies gave me extra large helpings!

Jade had a good day too. She'd learned a lot. She didn't try painting her feet, or playing in the mud or borrowing the hamster. Just to make sure she didn't forget, I made up a rap for her.

About the author

This is my third story
about Clive. This time we
meet his little sister. I got
the idea for this story
from one of the
illustrations that Dee
Shulman did in the first
Clive book (*Cool Clive*).

Dee drew a little sister in one of the
pictures and I thought to myself, 'I bet that
little sister is a bit of a pest...' Then I started
daydreaming around that idea. This story is
the result of those daydreams.